Bermuda Triangle's Most Wanted

Life on the Run

Bermuda Triangle's Most Wanted

Life on the Run

KENITH "ETHAN" BULFORD

StoryTerrace

Text Kenith Bulford and Bernard Bale, on behalf of StoryTerrace
Copyright © Kenith "Ethan" Bulford

First print June 2023

www.StoryTerrace.com

Some elements of this story have been fictionalised.

CONTENTS

1: WHY BOTHER?   11

2: WHEN I WAS JUST A KID   17

3: GROWING UP AND THE START OF A NEW 'CAREER'   27

4: RUNNING A BUSINESS AND RUNNING FROM THE POLICE   37

5: STILL RUNNING A BUSINESS BUT POLICE GET TOO CLOSE FOR COMFORT   43

6: LIVING IN AMERICA!   47

7: NEAR-DEATH EXPERIENCE   55

8: HERE WE GO AGAIN!!!   63

9: PETTY CRIMINAL TO PRIME SUSPECT   71

10: NO COMMENT!   79

11: NOT AGAIN!   85

12: TRYING TO PROVE MY INNOCENCE   89

13: MORE ARRESTS!	**95**
14: WINNING BIG 73K	**103**
15: CROWN AND ANCHOR	**109**
16: WHAT HAPPENED NEXT?	**119**
17: GONE FISHING - AND GOING STRAIGHT	**123**
IN CONCLUSION	**131**

1: WHY BOTHER?

Write a book? Are you crazy? No way in hell.

Yes, that's how I would have reacted when I was a kid living on my wits as well as on the streets. My mind was full of survival, stealing a bike and worse, I would not have been interested in writing a book. I'm not even sure I could read one, let alone write one!

So why the change? Why has this kid from Bermuda, who has spent much more time on the run than sitting under a cool fan in the library, and was more likely to be sitting under a palm tree smoking a joint, suddenly decided to become an author. An author? Really? Me? Wow, so I am.

Why the change? Because of you my friend, and your friends and your family. You see I know what it is like to always be looking over your shoulder, always keeping an eye on everyone around you because you cannot trust anyone. It is a living hell. I know what it's like to be in prison with the next guy wanting to prove something and the wardens wanting to prove even more.

I don't wish all that on anyone and if this book, my story, helps just one person to avoid all that, or get out of it if they are already in it, then that is mission accomplished, some guy I may never know not having to go through and take his family through days and nights of living a life of threatening shadows.

OK, sometimes it is exciting but most of the time it isn't, it is just fear for yourself and those that mean something to you.

Fear of what? Fear of who? This book will tell you all about that but let me tell you now, the person to really fear is yourself. Can you trust yourself to run on the right track? Can you trust yourself not to do something stupid?

Well, if you can't trust yourself, who can you trust? The simple answer is nobody, and after a while you learn to live with that and completely move away from any sort of normal friendships or family feeling. You have no idea of what you are missing and you don't want to know. You have friends – sort of. They are your friends while you are acceptable but can become your enemies at the drop of a dime.

Is that the kind of life you want? I tried to convince myself that I could live with that. I did live with that but it wasn't good. In fact it was very bad and I am so thankful that we are talking the past here not the present, and I pray that it is not the future.

You might think that this is some kind of lecture or a sermon to try and save people from themselves. It isn't. I am not trying to teach or preach, I am just sharing with you my life, which I guess can be described as 'adventurous'. Maybe there are other descriptions but I'll let you decide on that when you have been on the journey with me.

Yes, there has been fun some of the time. Some of that fun has been at other people's expense and you have the right to your own opinion, but I hope at least you will enjoy sharing the experiences of this boy from Bermuda who ducked and dived, ran and ran, braved things out at times and hid at other times.

I am not setting myself up as some kind of guru, saying "don't do as I did, do as I say." That is not what this is about, that is not what I am about. I just hope that some people who will suffer badly from living as I did will have something to think about *before* they get in over their heads.

How do I know all this? Well, I have been in and out of trouble for much of my life since I was just a little kid. Today I am a law-abiding citizen and I have a successful business. I am in my late 40s and I have a totally different life now.

My grandfather taught me fishing – he had a more relaxed approach to life. Perhaps I should have done more fishing when I was younger but maybe I will make up for it now that life has fewer shadows and a lot more sunshine.

I should have listened more to my grandfather. Instead my mentors, my advisors – my 'friends' – were drug dealers and other criminals. My home was the streets.

Yes I know that sounds like boasting or maybe seeking sympathy – it ain't any of that. It is just the facts of life – my life or rather my life for the early part of my life, if you see what I mean. It wasn't glamorous, it was dangerous but it did teach me a lot of lessons, which in writing this I am passing on to you.

So let's take the journey back, and walk the road to today and the here and now. I don't know if any of it will give you pleasure, but it is an adventure and prices have been paid.

The lessons are there for you if you want them, but if you just want an adventure then I am happy to share mine with you.

BERMUDA TRIANGLE'S MOST WANTED

I am nobody special, I am just Kenith Bulford – and this is my story.

2: WHEN I WAS JUST A KID

I was born in Bermuda. I guess I could say *on* the island of Bermuda but since Bermuda is made up of five main islands and more than a hundred small islands it is easier to say *in* Bermuda. If you have never been you are missing out on a treat because we have a sub-tropical climate, which means it is sunny and warm all the year round.

I don't want to sound like I am working for the Bermuda Tourist Office but it is beautiful and we don't have too much trouble from hurricanes. Because it is a small country most of the hurricanes miss us. We get some of the strong winds during the hurricane season but we never get the full force of the storms – I am pleased to say!

So there I was, born in hospital but growing up in what is best described as a Bermudian cottage on Somerset Island with my grandfather and grandma, my mama, her two brothers and sister. It was 'cosy', with basically two bedrooms, a kitchen and an outhouse. We had an ocean view, which sounds spectacular and I suppose it was, but most people in Bermuda have an ocean view so we kind of took it for granted, although living by the sea meant fishing.

My grandfather used to take me fishing from a very early age. He had fished all his life and really knew what to do, although he did kind of stray onto the wrong side of the law now and then. That was not as bad as it might sound. He simply kept up the old methods of pot fishing, which had been banned. Most of the time he got away with it, but sometimes the authorities would intervene and he would be told off or even fined. On one occasion, Grandpa and I had gone out fishing in his boat. Our goal was to catch a rockfish, and that was accomplished not long after we anchored off. Grandpa hooked a monster of a rockfish, so strong that it almost pulled him off the boat, and I had to grab hold of him for added support as he fought to reel it in. That was one of the biggest fish I have ever caught.

My grandfather taught me a lot about fishing, and even as a little boy I decided that I would be a fisherman when I grew up. I actually did but that is just one part of the story. My grandfather was also a drummer and, as you can imagine, there was always music all around us. In fact everywhere you went in Bermuda there was music – reggae and calypso were the most popular. There were radios and recorded music everywhere and, most of all, you would hear the music of Bob Marley.

So reggae was what you would hear in our home and next door, where we had more family. We had a lot of family in the area so it was a pretty good place to grow up. We ate a lot of seafood because there was so much of it readily available in the ocean and Grandpa was such an expert! I never knew much about my father but my grandfather was the best!

I learned to run errands from a very early age and 'running errands' would get me into trouble later on. Right now, the day dawned when I started school. I was not that keen, although I went to Somerset Primary School, which was a pretty good place and had been around for more than a hundred years. It looked like it too when I went to school, but it looks very modern now and has a good reputation.

People used to say I was lucky to go there – "it will be the best years of your life." I didn't believe them because I could not stand being told what to do and how to do it all the time. I was kind of a free spirit and liked to do my own thing. From a very early age I loved all kinds of sport – cricket, football, athletics, that kind of thing. I could spend all day doing sport and often did. My problem was that I was not an academic. I did not want to learn things that I could not see as having any particular value. It was OK at first, I was not bad at school, but bit by bit I grew to dislike it and did not study anything properly. By the time I had finished I hated it – except for sport.

While I was at primary school I was held back for a year because I was not as attentive to my school work as I should have been. It didn't help me, it just made me like school even less.

I must tell you about Ely's Harbour, the area I grew up in. It is a harbor but also a small town, and perfectly placed between the north-western tip of the mainland and the southern end of Somerset Island. It is a natural harbor set in the bay and, of course, great for fishing trips.

It is quite a naturally sheltered area because there are many small islands off the shore, including Morgan's Island and Bethell's Island. Great location and we have some great place names in Bermuda. For instance, quite near Ely's Harbour is Pilchard Bay. No prizes for guessing why it is called that.

So Ely's Harbour is where I grew up, among people who fished and had a lot of local crafts, which helped provide a living. There were – as everywhere – some places where groups could just hang out. When I was a little kid I soon got to know where those places were and the people who gathered in those places just to hang out. So I used to meet up with those guys while I was still very young.

I liked it and as I grew up I probably went to a favored place in Ely's Harbour more often. Then I went there through my teen years. It was just a place – a beautiful place – where you could hang out with others, talk, share thoughts, plot things depending on how old you were, oh yes and smoke things you didn't oughta smoke. Yes, I went there often and that's probably where I had my first smoke.

The first time I smoked weed I was eight years old. That was not uncommon in our part of the world. A lot of kids smoked something or other before they were into double figures. I remember taking a few puffs and feeling like I could take on the world, it was certainly a feeling like no other. Yes I was 'high and hungry'. I'm not promoting it. I'm not sure that it is the best thing for an eight-year-old kid, but it happened and it still happens.

Also, in a similar vein, when I was nine I was helping 'farm' a cannabis patch. The marijuana plants were taller than me, it was like working in a jungle!

The drugs scene at that time was pretty prominent in everyone's lives. Even if you had nothing to do with it you could find yourself caught up in a drug bust going down. There was always a drug lord who controlled a whole area.

Some stood out and were very well known. They usually got caught at some stage and ended up in jail.

When I was ten we moved home for a while but returned to Somerset a little later. It was not far away so we kept in touch with family and friends. I continued at school, although I didn't enjoy it except when we were playing sport. While at primary school I got into playing football and cricket and some athletics too. At last they – and I – found something I was good at.

We tried most things and I especially liked playing football, although we all loved cricket of course and it was rare that a match suffered from 'rain stopped play'. I developed as an athlete too, although I was still very young. I was good at high jump, long jump and middle-distance running. Since I used to naturally run a lot I enjoyed running for the school, just about the only thing I did like about school. It is probably fair to school that while I walked to school, when it was time to go home I ran!

I had a few friends at school and we used to hang around together as well as play sports. 'Hanging around' is a major pastime in Bermuda and can mean a lot of different things, not all of them good. By the time I was ready to go to my next school I was already pretty good at spending time with the older guys and getting involved in some of their pastimes. I was behind a bit at school but ahead of my years when it came to street 'cred'.

By the time I was 12 I was ready to move up a gear into a more senior school and probably more senior hanging around.

I have no complaints about Somerset Primary School. By the time I left there I had found sports, I had learned a few things but not as much as I should. I had worried my Mum when I was kept back a year because of my bad school report. I had discovered that I was really good at some things but they were mostly to do with sports and fishing.

My future was already being shaped by my environment and the people I hung out with. Little did I know that some of the things I was learning then would actually provide me with the craft to walk on the wrong side of the law as I grew up. I had spent time at the primary school learning the basics of life so when I left I was a much more experienced kid than when I started – I had also lost my virginity. I remember that day so vividly. The girl had recently moved to Bermuda from the US, she had red hair and the body of an adult woman. Beautiful was an understatement. During the lunch period my friend and I took turns having sex with her in the tall thick oleander bushes. She was two years older than us so she took the lead. I would like to think she was proud to make me a man.

I had become a man of the world even before my teens.

3: GROWING UP AND THE START OF A NEW 'CAREER'

The sun never stopped shining and I never stopped running, playing football and cricket and kind of enjoying myself, except that I finally moved to a new school and found the same old problem – I was never going to be an academic. I knew I ought to have a better attitude but I just couldn't seem to listen to my own advice.

It was mostly boring and I preferred sport, music and hanging out with friends. I went to Sandy's Secondary School and it wasn't that I hated it, I actually quite liked it. But I had no great ambition to be a doctor or a lawyer, the kind of careers that everyone else seemed to want. My ambition for a long time had been to have my own fishing business – that was it, nothing else.

To be honest, that has never really changed and to an extent I have achieved that, but there has been so much more in my life that I felt I had to write this book to signpost to others what kind of a journey it can be.

These days I can put my hand on my heart and tell you that I am a law-abiding citizen and, dare I say it, a successful businessman. But it didn't start like that and if I can help people find their direction without doing some of the wrong things I did then that's great. The trouble is that you can fall into this trap without even realising it. What starts as a bit of fun, a bit of showing off, soon becomes a way of life, as you will see.

With my teen years came a change of friends and companions and a change of outlook, partly influenced by those I spent most of my time hanging out with. I'll let you, the reader, be the judge of whether this was a good time in my life or not, but my own experience is that the teen years are a launching pad to the path your life is likely to follow.

At school I once again found myself held back for a year. I am not going to blame the school but perhaps we could all have done better. I could have had a better attitude and realised that there was more to life than sport and hanging out with friends, but maybe the school could have done better in realising that I was someone who needed that little bit of extra help and understanding. Whatever, it was not a great experience and with home life being short of a definable leadership my friends became my mentors – not a great idea really.

This is probably a good time to mention that when I was still very young I was shot in the arm! That sounds very dramatic but it was an accident, although a pretty stupid one. I'll explain.

I used to hang out with street guys on an area of the beach that nobody went to. I started smoking weed when I was very young and I guess that since I was hanging out with guys who were older than me I started to feel grown-up. It never occurred to me that perhaps the older guys also needed to do some growing up. To me they were street-wise and I was just glad to be accepted by them. They knew where I was and I did little jobs like running errands for them – usually to do with drugs. They became a second family to me and I was impressed by their attitude, bravado and fun.

When it was a bit cold – by Bermuda standards – we used to light a fire on the beach. One time someone had a box of bullets and we all thought it would be a great idea to tip some bullets onto the fire and see what happened. We soon found out as they started to explode and fire off in all directions. Two of them came in my direction; one slightly grazed my forehead and the other lodged into my left arm. Suddenly it was no longer funny.

My pals patched it up with something that did the job of a bandage but probably would have sent medical people into shock. They took me home with blood dripping from my wound. My mother freaked out, as you can imagine, but she did what mothers do and cleaned the wound and dressed it properly. She was none too impressed with what had happened. I had to tell her the truth because she had a way of always knowing when I was lying or attempting to mislead her. She made sure I was OK first and then told me off. She did a good job but of course the bullet was never removed which means that I still have it in my arm as a souvenir to this very day! It's not like a tattoo, people kinda have to take your word for it.

By now you will probably have the idea that I was a pretty useless kid but it was not entirely like that. I was good at some things, like athletics, and I was also a pretty good pump attendant. I got a part-time job at a gas station when I was 15 and did that for about 18 months. It brought a bit of money into my pocket and also some for my family. Yes, I was close to feral but I still had my family.

Also during this time some of the guys started to call me 'Ethan'. I never knew why but it stuck so friends often call me Ethan today, although it is not anything to do with my real name.

So I left school at 15, still had the job at the gas station but needed something better. That is when I became a construction worker. I couldn't do anything that needed skill but I was a good labourer where only brawn was required.

Even then I supplemented my earnings with a few other regular jobs. What were they? They were a gateway to what was to come because I started doing more than running errands with drugs, I began selling them myself, as well as getting into petty crime such as stealing bikes and the like. One time just after stealing a bike I was heading home and ran into a police stop and search. Immediately, I knew attempting to cross it ran too much risk. First of all, the bike I was riding was stolen, and I also had weed in my jacket pocket. In an effort to avoid getting caught I made a sudden U-turn in the road. The police saw my turn and began to follow me. I led them on a high-speed chase for a few minutes until I no longer saw them behind me. I hid in a ravine overnight until I was certain they were gone. The next morning, I woke up riddled by mosquito bites – but I managed to hold on to my bike.

The trouble with that kind of thing is that it solves immediate problems and after a while it becomes second nature. It does not take very long before you almost see it as your job, and the risks involved find their way to the back of your mind instead of the front. You don't even think about the consequences to yourself or others. It becomes just what you do. Some people play a guitar or work in a bank – I sell drugs and steal bikes and things.

I guess you could say it was a career move, but not the best. Looking back at it, yes I made money and I had fun but there was always going to be a price to pay.

4: RUNNING A BUSINESS AND RUNNING FROM THE POLICE

As I said, I left school at 15 and worked in the gas station full-time, well sort of full-time. I had a part-time business on the streets and that was going quite well. Then came the construction job I moved on to when I was 16.

I had no construction skills at all so I just did laboring. That was OK because it meant that I was very fit, which was just as well since my part-time business sometimes called for fitness!

Perhaps at this stage I should explain that at the age of 17 I also became a dad. I was only a kid myself of course but I was and still am proud of my first son. It is not unusual in Caribbean and other cultures for mid-teenagers to become parents and the whole family get involved in bringing up children, so there is a good family atmosphere from the start.

Anyway, after eight months as a construction worker I decided that I should go full-time on my street sales. I had been dabbling but wanted to move up a gear. It was not difficult to achieve.

How it worked was very simple – I knew dealers because I had worked for them, now it was just a change of relationship. Instead of running for them I would buy from them and sell on. They were happy because it increased their turnover and provided they were paid at the time they handed over drugs they were cool with it. From my point of view it was great because dealing meant that you basically doubled your money.

I know that sounds simple and it is in theory but there are always complications and I was very aware of the dangers, some of which came from the police of course.

The first rule of drug dealing or running was never get caught with any on you. We used to stash some stuff in the trees at the cricket and football ground where we used to hang out, so that if something went wrong we did not have anything in our pockets to incriminate us. Some would have a hole in the ground that was easily covered, and would hide stuff in there until it was needed.

The Naval Field was where people gathered for some sport or just recreation, but I used to hang out with my friends and do business there. Most of our customers were locals but you used to also get crew and others from the ships that were docked nearby.

The police used to swoop on us fairly regularly. It was different in those days. Today the police have to be more respectful, more patient and helpful in some ways. When I was younger they were much harder and would clamp down by being physically and verbally aggressive, sometimes very aggressive.

They used to appear from nowhere like storm troopers and shout at you and hit you. I used to find myself especially targeted for some reason. I never answered back or tried to be aggressive in return. I just did my best to keep a low profile and accept whatever would happen. During one incident, the police had been watching us selling drugs by Somerset Cricket

Club. Once they decided to bust us they snatched me up first, throwing me into the back of the police car and splitting my lip in the process. They transported me back to Somerset Police Station but taking the scenic route. At this point I knew what this meant – they stopped mid-way and beat the shit out of me. I was left with bruises, a broken nose, and black eyes. Normally if you resisted you just caused more trouble for yourself. I was unlucky because I had not resisted in any way.

There were other problems too, not often, but occasionally you would have trouble with a customer. I remember one guy let me know he wanted some of what I had. We agreed a price and I was just handing his order over to him when I realised he was trying to cheat me. It was an old trick that some tried with paper money. They fold it so that it looks more than it actually is. This guy passed me some folded notes as I was passing him his order. It did not feel right to me and when I looked at the cash he was giving me it was about half what it was supposed to be. So I would not let go of the drugs. He tried to wrestle them from me but I held on. That turned into a full-scale altercation and would not be the last. I didn't lose my wares though.

Today the police seem to be much more lenient and the raids are much fewer. In my day we used to get raided half a dozen times in as many days. I gather that today the police have a much lower profile. They used to hide and watch us for some time before they pounced. I think there is a case for a better cooling off period, especially now when times are hard all over the world and people turn to crime as a last resort.

I must tell you right now that I have never actually used drugs myself except for smoking marijuana, but one occasion nearly changed that. It was late in the evening and I was just about to conclude a transaction, which meant I would be selling some 'crack' to a customer. We were in the park and the police just appeared from nowhere. Everywhere I ran the gates were firmly closed and guarded. They had caught me but they didn't see the block of crack I had in my hand. I didn't know what to do with it and being caught would have meant going to jail so I didn't see that I had any choice but to swallow the stuff.

They didn't see me do it but within a few minutes I was as high as a kite and felt dreadful. I couldn't stand up straight, I made no sense when I spoke. They probably guessed what I had done but they couldn't prove anything. The law was that you had to be caught with the stuff *on* you not *in* you.

I really felt bad though, and it took me a couple of hours before I started to come down. I vowed never to do that again. People call them recreational drugs but that crack cocaine did not seem much fun to me.

It was not only drugs we sold on the streets – we sold clothes too. Along with a friend I got a peddler's licence and we used to buy jeans, T-shirts and other clothing wholesale from New York and then we had a regular place on the street and used a wall as our shelving. That worked for about three years, from when I was 18 until I was 21. It was good business, we still sold cheap but we had been able to buy cheap so everyone was happy.

After I left the construction laboring work I never got another job. I have lived on my wits ever since, sometimes successfully and sometimes... well, in trouble.

Of course I have some regrets, but I just did what I needed to do to survive and to try to make some progress in life.

I look back and smile at some of those adventures and also some of the fun we had. Some friends and I went by regular flight to New York and also by charter flight to Jamaica for a holiday. It was great and we used to party from day one until we got back, usually about two weeks later. Happy days.

There were more happy days to come and also some which were pretty traumatic, but that was in the future. For that moment I was leaving my teens behind and I had become an entrepreneur of the streets. I dabbled in crime, my friends dabbled in crime and I was a target for the police. I am not boasting about that, it was just a way of life I found myself in. It got worse before it got better.

5: STILL RUNNING A BUSINESS BUT POLICE GET TOO CLOSE FOR COMFORT

Those close encounters with the police did not end, quite the opposite – they got hotter! There I was making money from selling drugs, mostly those I had bought from a wholesaler but sometimes on behalf of someone else. The clothes business was another hustle which earned some money, not as much as the drugs but enough for us to keep it going for about three years.

Looking back to before I was 21, I had a very active life. I made my first trip to New York – Brooklyn to be exact – when I was 16. I had a friend there from Bermuda. That first trip was great, the second trip when I was 17 was not so great. Let me tell you about that!

I was standing outside the Chinese corner store with my friend when suddenly a guy appeared and waved a gun at us both before shooting in our direction. Our initial reaction was to take cover behind a parked car. Soon after my friend pulled his gun and began firing back. There was a full-scale shootout and I was stuck in the middle of it. Ultimately, my friend was shot in the foot and the rival shooter was shot in his shoulder and abdomen. Then he made off in a car and we had to get my friend to hospital quickly. They patched up his foot, removed some shrapnel from it and he was allowed to go home.

I didn't really know what any of that was about until my friend explained that he had had an altercation with the guy and it came to blows. My boy got the best of it and the point was made or so he thought. The shooting was a warning. That was not the end of the story though, because as soon as he could, my friend went looking for the guy. I didn't know what to expect but when they met up they just discussed their difference of opinion and reached an agreement. If only it was always that simple.

I was no stranger to guns so I was not in a state of shock, but when it was pointed at me for a few seconds it did make me think a little. Just for the record, I fired a gun for the first time when I was 16. Some of the guys I used to hang around with had guns. I didn't have one myself but they used to let us handle theirs.

Back in Bermuda I had, as I have mentioned, had run-ins with the police, who went through phases of tackling drug use and sales. The first time I was caught with crack cocaine was when I was 17. Gun Alley was one area where we used to hang out and sell, sometimes to local people but also often to tourists. I was one of the younger guys and there were others in their twenties. There was an apartment there where a guy sold drugs wholesale. I visited there and bought three rocks, which I put in my pocket, and then got talking so I forgot they were there.

I left the apartment and walked across the road to the trees where we used to hang out and suddenly the narcotics police arrived. I was stopped and searched and there were the three blocks of crack cocaine. I was so annoyed with myself. I could have thrown them away but no, I was just plain dumb.

So I was shoved into a police car and they didn't care about you banging your head, or them banging your head for you. I was roughed up a bit at the police station too and eventually charged with possession. I was bailed and it took more than a year to come to court. I kept putting it back with various excuses, but in the end I decided to plead guilty to possession of Class A drugs. As far as anyone was concerned I had them for myself so I was guilty of possession rather than supplying. I was fined a couple of hundred dollars and warned as to my future conduct.

On other occasions that I was arrested it was usually for assaulting a police officer. Sometimes I got away, especially if I had a bike, but sometimes not. They could rough you up as much as they liked but if you pushed one of them away to protect yourself you were alleged to have assaulted them. So the police and I got to know each other – we didn't actually become friends but we did get to know each other.

My lifestyle changed of course. One way or another I was making money so I used to treat myself. I started to buy expensive clothes, I like motorbikes so I bought a couple of those for use on the road and also motocross bikes for fun, and eventually I bought a car, which was just great. It was not spectacular – a Suzuki J10. It was green and quite small, but it was my first car and I was pretty proud of it.

I used to travel places for fun as well as business, and all in all I had a pretty good life on an island that was very beautiful. I loved the sea and to have this beautiful ocean all around me was great. I never took it for granted.

My son's mother and I were together for about three years but then we drifted apart, so I didn't have a regular girlfriend for a while and just met girls as I traveled around.

Despite the efforts of the police, I and guys like me made a good living. We were committed to what we were doing. At that stage I don't think I could have gone back to construction work or the gas station. We had a much more rewarding career and enjoyed those rewards to the full. I don't think any of us saved for the future. We lived for now. We had fun and even when the police were coming onto our patch that was more exciting than anything else. Trying to outwit them, outrun them and generally keep ahead of the game had an element of fun which is hard to describe if you haven't experienced it. If you were caught you accepted whatever came your way but if you escaped you saw the fun side of it – maybe that was just relief!

I must say that I am not saying this to encourage others to do the same. This is how my life developed. I have a few regrets but regrets do not change history, and I am just telling what it was like to be me during those years.

The police were a constant threat, never far away, but we still managed to ply our trade. Apart from an occasional problem we kept ahead of the game – or at least we did until reinforcements came from the US and suddenly my life changed once again. This easy-going way of life I was leading was about to become not so easy-going.

6: LIVING IN AMERICA!

I had been visiting America now and then for a number of years, but there was a vast difference between planning a trip and having a trip forced upon you. Well, that is what happened.

Around the beginning of 1997 the government of Bermuda decided to get more serious in its clampdown on drugs and drug sales. The US offered help and sent a small army of their Drug Enforcement Agents, people that we, of course, did not know.

They didn't swoop in like a SWAT team, they were much more subtle than that.

They were all equipped with little motorbikes, more like scooters, and traveled around certain designated areas of Bermuda. They had the usual helmets, which meant that you could not see their faces very well. They carried out surveillance operations for some time before they took action.

We were local, we knew local people and we knew local police so we could see a situation coming and get prepared for it. The DEA agents were different, they just rode around and made approaches to people, almost like tourists on hire bikes looking to buy some stuff. Some came to us two or three times so we were getting used to seeing them, still not realizing who they were. We were used to having regular customers but also tourists, so we were off-guard with these guys.

I mostly stuck with selling crack cocaine, but on one occasion while these guys were around I was asked to sell some heroin for someone else.

Anyway, I was on the street and selling. One of my cousins was with me, he had come along just for a chat. While he was there he helped me with a customer. The heroin was in a plastic bag and I had to scoop some out to put into another, smaller bag for the customer.

My cousin handed the customer his little plastic bag of heroin and life went on – or so we thought. Three weeks later my cousin was arrested. Meanwhile I just continued supplying. The clampdown was under way. Multiple people were caught, I think the figure was around 45 and mostly from the Somerset area. They were clamping down on sales, not so much on possession.

So I was overlooked but I knew it would not be for long. I was known to them so it was only going to be a matter of time. I was worried of course, and didn't really know what to do. I decided that it was time to leave the country, and went immediately. Of everyone involved from my neighborhood I was the only one to evade this operation. Some of those arrested were getting up to three years in jail and I didn't like the sound of that.

I caught a flight to Philadelphia. I had been before but this was a little more urgently. I made it to the US, and I had not been there very long before a friend got in touch and told me that there had been an increase in police activity and more arrests by undercover cops, some of whom were even inside the jail to get more information. He told me that I was on tape so I must have been approached by them when I was selling and they had recorded the conversation.

This was really the first time I had ever been on the run like this and it was not a great position to be in. I didn't go anywhere very much in case I was recognized. I knew a few people and they let me sleep at their place until I found something of my own. In the end a friend's mother let me have a room for as long as it was needed and this how I came to live in Harlem, at the well-known Wagner Projects.

If you have never been to Harlem, let me explain that there are two sides to it. One is the rough side and the other is the very rough side. The Blood gang reigned supreme but there were many others, even of the Blood chapter. I stayed inside a lot of the time but there were a few close calls. For some there was a resentment that I was from Bermuda. I kept a low profile mostly, although I did keep some acquaintances who helped me stay out of trouble.

I think it is fair to say that Harlem was pretty crazy. It is not a huge area but it is pretty busy with a big population and rival gangs. I found that there were a lot more people carrying knives and even machetes. Guns were also more plentiful than I had experienced before. Gangs used to meet on the outdoor public basketball courts to discuss business and territorial agreements. That said, there was a pretty relaxed atmosphere a lot of the time.

One incident I recall was when I was invited to a party by a new friend who always carried a shotgun. The party was at a small club and when we arrived my pal hid his shotgun down his trousers – it was fully long-barreled, not one that had been sawed. He actually managed to sneak it in, but all was revealed when he had to adjust it to stop the gun from falling down his leg and ended up shooting himself in the calf. The whole club scattered after hearing the shot, it was total mayhem. We were left in the middle of the dance floor with a chunk of flesh missing and a pool of blood. Another trip to hospital!

Yes. it was an odd place to be – not just because it was Harlem but also because this was a new experience for me. I did not like having to keep quiet. I had always been an 'out there' kind of guy but now I was having keep a very low profile. I must confess though, that for all the back-watching it was still a very exciting time and I got a kind of buzz from constantly having to be careful.

I made a few new friends, and had some that I had known from Bermuda, in particular my second child's mother. We lived together for a few months. She then moved to New Jersey, where she later gave birth to our lovely daughter, and in 2002 I became the proud father of a second son.

So I lived in New Jersey for a couple of years too. Friends and family from Bermuda came to visit me. I missed them a lot so it was always really good to see them again. It is worth remembering that I was in the US illegally, I had no work permit or anything so I had to keep a low profile. One of my favorite pastimes was the strip club – being a young man, my hormones often got the best of me. My favorite strip club was called Brown Derby. After one night out with some Bermudan friends there was another club shooting – it started to feel like every time I went out someone was shot. On this particular night as we were leaving gun shots rang out, and just as I approached the exit a man dropped at my feet. I remember stopping in my tracks looking at him and all around me before making my exit. That was the last time I went there.

I worked as I had in Bermuda – buying and selling on the streets and making a few dollars where I could. It was OK and I was doing fine but I had been away from Bermuda for a number of years – seven I think. I missed the place and I decided to take a chance and return home. By now they would have forgotten all about me and I could pick up the pieces again.

Yes, I was resolved, I was heading back to my roots, beautiful Bermuda.

7: NEAR-DEATH EXPERIENCE

It was great to be back with my family and friends, but this was not the same Bermuda I had left some years ago. There had been an increase in the gang culture and it began to change the social climate. After a month I was in trouble again and this time it was very serious. Because of a mix-up I found myself under arrest on suspicion of murder. Yes, really! Murder. I could not believe it but the police insisted I went with them and I knew they wouldn't take no for an answer.

I was 'helped' into the back of a police van and taken off to the local police station. I was allowed to phone a lawyer, who came straight away and told me to say nothing. I took his advice and the only two words I used were 'no comment'. Because they could not actually jail me at that stage, I was released on a $5,000 bail. I was told to report back in one month. I nodded in agreement but I was already formulating other plans.

I didn't see any alternative to fleeing the island once again but it was going to take some planning. So I went into hiding and was helped by friends and family who believed in my innocence. I had a boat – my own sailing boat – but I needed a captain, someone who knew about navigating.

We did find someone but he was taking his time in deciding whether to take up the offer. I think that the 'wanted' notices that went up all over the island when I failed to turn up to answer my bail made him at least a little nervous. I was starting to get nervous myself because the hurricane season would soon be upon us, and that would make it almost impossible to leave the island in a sailing boat. A submarine would have been useful but I didn't have one of those!

My captain pulled out, which was disappointing but I understood his dilemma. I decided to phone some friends overseas and one of them knew just the right person. He was an experienced captain and we agreed terms. With the help of friends I booked him an airline ticket and a few days later he landed on Bermuda in time for us to miss the hurricane season. I was really pleased about that because the season usually runs from June to the beginning of December, and that would have meant about six months more in hiding.

He needed about 10 days to get familiar with the boat, because his experience as a captain was with motorized vessels and my boat was all sails.

I had been sailing boats since I was a kid so I had a pretty good knowledge of how to do it, but I knew nothing about navigation, sea lanes or anything like that. Between us we worked out how we were going to do it, and I guess we were teaching each other.

Late one night we slipped out of the mangrove area and we were on our way. I was very relieved, but I might not have been had I known what was ahead.

The first three days at sea were great. We made steady progress and had time for a beer or two and some relaxation. For me it was especially good because I was out of hiding and more or less out of reach. Then it all changed as we were hit by some really stormy weather. The waves built up to about

35 feet and were slapping the side of the boat, sounding like cannons being fired. Scared? Absolutely! I was terrified, especially when the boat keeled over and went totally upside down. Sailing boats are built to be able to tip themselves back upright and ours did. We were so grateful that we had remembered to bolt every window and door so that the water couldn't get in, otherwise we would have sunk for sure. As it was we were upright, still being hammered by the storm, and our supplies were strewn all over the floor inside the cabin. We were still alive though, and slowly the storm calmed. We tidied up and pushed on, with a fair wind helping us.

There was still another problem, a very personal one.

I had not been to the bathroom for some time. I thought maybe I had locked up because of the storms but that wasn't the case. I had a stomach ache which was getting progressively worse and I stopped eating. I started to feel sick and I felt full, very full. It was very worrying because I really felt myself getting quite ill – very unusual for me. I started to feel like I was going to die. I know that sounds dramatic but really that is how I felt. Both my captain and I knew we had to get help from somewhere.

There was a small island within reach so we changed direction and headed for that, and when we finally arrived there we anchored off and took our small dinghy to the shore. There were only a few people around but a guy gave us a lift to the town. We were also in need of new batteries for the boat and we found those quite easily. Getting medical attention was more difficult.

As strangers we were not very welcome to simply come ashore and ask for medical help, it was very limited and the locals, understandably, put their own needs above those of strangers. I was getting desperate and then got talking to a guy who told me two buy two Club Sodas. I thought he was crazy but I was at the point where I would try just about anything.

So I bought two Club Sodas and drank them one after the other. We were back on the boat by now and guess what – nothing happened. At least, nothing happened for half an hour, and then I felt something starting to stir inside me. I quickly went to the back of the boat and swung over the side so I was in position to do what I hoped I was going to do. Sure enough it worked! And it worked! And it worked! Without going into too much detail I could tell from the colours and the aromas that this was serious stuff and I had been close to being poisoned. So let's hear it for Club Soda!

Two days later we were at our destination, and we arrived in broad daylight at what looked to be a busy time. We couldn't just turn up as if we were expected so once again we anchored and took our dinghy to the shore. There were fisherman about and some other people clearly saw us, which was not great news. We didn't want to attract attention but we did, and we could see some military getting interested in us.

We headed for woodland, jumped off the little boat and ran into the forest. I couldn't believe that they actually ran after us and then opened fire. What a welcome – bullets were flying around us as we ran for cover. They eventually gave up on us but we saw that they had seized our boat, so we were glad we had brought the important things with us.

We waited until evening and then left the woods and managed to get a lift to another area of the island, where we were able to get somewhere to stay, hot food, a bath and even some recreation time. That would do us nicely for a couple of days.

 **Bermuda Police Service**

$5,000 REWARD

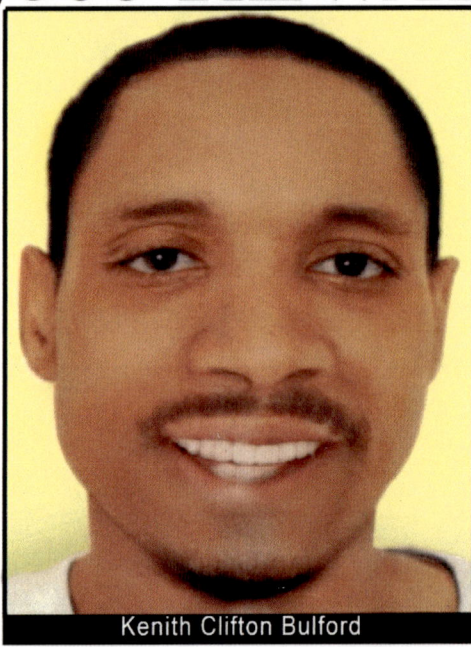
Kenith Clifton Bulford

The Commissioner of Police is appealing to the public for information regarding the whereabouts of this man: **Kenith Clifton Bulford.** Mr. Bulford or "Ethan" as he is also called, is described as 6 feet 4 inches tall, brown skinned, of medium build, weighing approximately 180 to 200 pounds. He is wanted in connection with offences under the Firearms Act. Anyone with information about this individual is actively encouraged to contact Police or the Crime Stoppers 24 hour confidential hotline on 1-800-623-8477.

A reminder that any information received will be treated in the strictest of confidence, and a reward of $5,000 is offered for any information leading to his arrest.

8: HERE WE GO AGAIN!!!

Two days of comfort were great but there was still the need to move on and get off the island. I had a passport so that should be OK, hopefully. The captain and I parted company, I paid him, thanked him from the bottom of my heart and bought us two airline tickets. We were going to different places, so different flights and different flight times. That was the end of our adventure together, and now it was up to me again to get to the airport and catch a flight out of there.

I checked in and that was where the trouble started – again! This was not an English-speaking island so that didn't help. A lady who was attached to immigration looked at my passport picture and didn't think it matched me so she took me to five immigration guys at a table – one of them seated and obviously in charge. There was a pile of wanted posters which they were looking at, and I guessed I would be among them. I was really nervous but I knew I had to be calm and react as any innocent person might.

"What's going on here man?" I asked. "You've made me miss my flight? Anyone here speak English?"

I wasn't aggressive but straight to the point and it worked. The guy in charge gave me back my passport, apologized for any inconvenience and arranged for me to catch a flight the next day. So I checked into a nearby motel for the night and went back the next day wondering what was going to happen this time.

BERMUDA TRIANGLE'S MOST WANTED

The answer was – nothing. All went smoothly and I was pretty happy when the plane finally got its wheels off the ground and I was heading for Jamaica. I relaxed again for the flight but the nerves started to jangle a little when we touched down and I had to go through another immigration barrier. The lady looked at my passport, looked at me, looked back at the passport, looked at me again and the said – "Welcome to Jamaica Sir". I was so relieved. It was a beautiful feeling.

I might as well tell you now that it was not my passport. The guy in the picture looked quite a lot like me but it wasn't me and, of course, the name wasn't mine.

I knew one or two people in Jamaica so I made some calls and found myself a room to rent with everything included. I kept a fairly low profile, in part because I had not been there very long when Hurricane Ivan struck!

It was 2004 when Ivan raged for two days – September 11 and 12, and its center passed near Jamaica without making a direct hit. Passing by was enough to cause a lot of damage though. There were 17 people killed and 18,000 left homeless. All the hotels and places opened again after a couple of days but there was so much damage, and most of all it knocked out the water supply.

It was incredible that as I holed up in my room I could hear gun shots as the police and military had battles with the various gangs in the area who were taking advantage of the hurricane weather to go looting. Gun shots were not rare in this part of Kingston, in fact I was living in a kind of ghetto area which was rough, and all the better for staying in my room a lot of the time.

The water supply was off for days and it became a very serious situation as people roamed trying to find water. One afternoon a cry went up that there was a water truck coming down the road. I grabbed a large bowl and others grabbed whatever they could find that would hold water. We all rushed out into the street and sure enough there was the water truck. It had armed soldiers all over it and did not actually stop, but traveled slowly for people to get what they could without it coming to a halt. There was a queue and the queue was moving with the truck. I have never seen such high security for water before or since!

I spent much of my time in my room but I exercised a lot and was in pretty good shape. I had some social life but I always knew that the day would come when I would have to leave here and start life again. It happened in a very unexpected way.

I met a guy briefly and found that he kept looking at me as if he was kind of studying me. He asked where I was from and I told him that I was born in Jamaica, spent a lot of time in the US and recently returned to Jamaica, which is why my accent was a bit different. He mentioned Bermuda but I told him that I didn't know anyone in Bermuda. It was nothing really but it worried me just a little.

On this particular day I woke up with an uneasy feeling, I felt as if my run was about to be cut short, so I needed to sort a few things out just in case my intuition was correct. Anyway, I had a girlfriend or something like that I had called and asked her to come over. I needed to relieve myself just in case it would be a while before having the opportunity to do so again.

She came over about 2 pm that day, dressed like she knew what was on my mind. Almost immediately we started kissing and touching each other, all while in the back of my mind I felt like the end was near. Something told me I had better make this worth it. I had her bent over my bed with a fist full of hair screwing her like this was the last time I would have sex in my life. As she moaned in pleasure I heard a loud bang at the door. I refused to stop, and kept pumping as she kept screaming! Just as we both climaxed my door was kicked in.

I covered myself with a sheet and jumped out of bed to ask who it was, although I had a feeling I knew exactly who it was.

"Who is it?" I demanded.

"Just open the door!" came a voice. I opened the door just a crack and immediately it was pushed open further and there were six guys with handguns pointed at my head and various other parts of my body. Next thing the door was completely burst open and they piled in, and the leading officer beat me in my upper torso with a machine gun. The girl began to scream. It was total pandemonium.

They showed me a poster of myself and told me they thought I was Kenith Bulford. I denied it was me. My hair had grown and I had plaits. They were not totally sure it was me but this was the flying squad and with them was a well-known Jamaican policeman everyone called Biggerford. They had a reputation. About 30-40% of the people they arrested were taken into custody, anyone who resisted was shot and never made it into custody.

I was allowed to get dressed and then someone said, "OK, let's go." There were no handcuffs but they tied my hands behind my back with one of my own belts. These guys did not bother with handcuffs. You either walked with them or you didn't walk ever again.

They arrested the girl too but we were separated, and I heard they let her go as soon as they had asked her a few questions about me.

On one occasion before all this took place I had been stopped and searched by police when I had a small amount of weed on my person. I was able to pay off the officers to avoid prosecution and immigration checks. They thought I was from Guyana, which worked in my favor as I was a wanted man. Ultimately they gave me back my weed and I was free to go.

That was so different. This time I was taken to downtown Kingston, where there was quite an entourage waiting to guard me. When I went inside there was a huge poster with the word WANTED in very big print over my photo. Everywhere I was taken I was surrounded by a group of armed police.

I didn't say very much, even when they studied my nose and said it was the same nose as in the photo on the poster. I was aware that someone had phoned through to Bermuda too. The odds were stacking up against me but I still said very little. The phone calls ended up with the police in Bermuda sending my fingerprints by fax.

So my fingerprints were taken and examined under some glass so that they were magnified. Their expert studied every little bit and then confirmed that I was indeed Kenith Bulford.

So I knew it was over and I asked to phone my lawyer. I knew his number well enough because I had been in touch with him so many times. I got through to him and he told me to sit tight and say nothing and he would put me in touch with someone else who was already in Jamaica. That man was Frank Phipps QC. He called me and said the same thing and that he would be on his way.

So I was taken to Central Police Station for one night before moving elsewhere. I sat in the cell and pondered what had happened in recent times. I had made a bid for freedom and succeeded for a while but then here I was, behind bars again and still with a potential murder charge hanging over my head.

9: PETTY CRIMINAL TO PRIME SUSPECT

I was only in the police station for one night and then I was taken to what is called South Camp but is better known as Gun Court, because it is both a prison and a court. It is well known in Jamaica since it was originally opened to try to reduce violent crime involving firearms in the country. It had a system in which one magistrate could sit and judge and issue prison sentences – it was like conveyor belt justice.

I was taken there with an armed guard and it was not long before I was in a cell, and was surprised to find another guy from Bermuda. He told me that he was there because they were trying to extradite him back to Bermuda for trying to get a cop killed. We were not in the same cell for long before I was moved to the cell next to him.

I was in Gun Court for just under a month and it was frustrating, but we were all cheered up when Jamaican reggae star Sizzla joined us. What a great character. He was brought in after being arrested for singing anti-gay and anti-establishment songs in his set. He brought the place to life because during the couple of days that he was there it was like a non-stop concert. We were all singing and dancing and making the best of our situation. Sizzla was taken away after those two days, and we were sorry to see him go but pleased that he was getting back to life on the outside.

I have to say that South Camp was pretty bad. We had no toilets in our cells and had to be taken outside. At night they would not let that happen so we were using plastic bags and had to just tie them up until we could get rid of them in the morning. The food was very poor and apart from Sizzla it was a horrible experience.

It was a relief to be sent to Horizon Remand Centre, which was much more humane, newer and compared to Gun Court was like an hotel. After three weeks I appeared in court and was charged with possession of a half-ounce of marijuana and illegal entry. I pleaded guilty but then had to wait to be sentenced.

I was in one big cell with a number of guys and because of that it was not unusual for fights to break out. They did not last long usually, although there was a stabbing on one occasion. One early morning, two inmates began arguing over a pair of sneakers. It eventually lead to blows, and suddenly an inmate produced a knife and slashed his opponents face and neck. There was blood all over everyone and everything. I was certain he would not survive, but he did. I had one or two altercations myself but nothing to get excited about. There was one occasion when the guards came in to sort something and one of the guys sniggered. They beat the hell out of him for that. I also had the privilege of meeting reggae artist Jah-Cure, who was in jail at the time.

After a few more weeks it was time to go back to court for sentencing and there were several of us going at the same time. We were loaded into a truck, which had individual cells in it, and we had an armed escort. We were soon at the Half-way Tree Court, another establishment that had a jail attached.

There were a lot of high-profile guys in the court that day so there were plenty of guards about. I actually felt quite small fry when I was handed a four-month sentence with a month knocked off for the time I had already served. The bad news was that my time was to be spent in the Half-way Tree jail, which was really terrible.

It made anything I had experienced before seem like a holiday. There were no bunks, just paper on the concrete floor. The bathroom was outside again so that was pretty bad, and the food consisted of chicken's feet and rice. I ate a lot of rice as there was no way I could eat chicken's feet.

The mood inside there was intense and you felt that anything could happen at any time. I did my best to work out a lot to try to keep myself in shape. I had one minor altercation but generally I was left alone. But you could not turn your back on anyone, inmates nor guards. Most of the guys in there had gun shot wounds, and one or two had multiple wounds from being shot and stabbed.

There was a lot of prejudice in there. Much depended on where they came from, what gang you had been with and so on. There was one guard who was OK. He used to get me a few things to make the stay better. I would give him some money and the deal was that he kept nearly half of it and spent the rest on things I needed.

Even so, I was counting the days until I got out and eventually that day came. I had served my time and that was the end of it.

Actually, no. That was the end of that matter but the bigger problem was still hanging over me. I was not actually released because I was immediately rearrested. Bermuda wanted me back because I still had the major accusation to answer. My wanted posters were still all over Bermuda and elsewhere – including Jamaica.

This is probably a good time to explain what the case was about. As mentioned, I was a prime suspect in a murder. It was all based on someone handing in a gun that had been used and saying that it was mine. They were prepared to give evidence that would tie me into having murdered someone.

Yes, this was serious stuff, very serious.

Of course I had been living with this ever since I had left Bermuda in the sailing boat, but the passage of time means that you can put it out of your mind more often. It doesn't make it go away though. The Jamaican police and the Bermudian police talked to each other, and I was going to be extradited.

Was I guilty or even involved? Well the answer to that will come out shortly but perhaps you would like to take a guess at it yourself. All I can tell you right now is that suddenly I went from small time to big time. I was prime suspect in a murder and that made me dangerous, even though I was still the same guy who had been inside for having a half-ounce of weed.

Before I was taken away again I gave some clothes and stuff to the other guys I had been in jail with, and also a special gift of a handcuff key I had acquired. Don't ask me how and don't ask me where I hid it when I was being searched. I just had it and was able to pass it on to someone else.

Early in the morning I was taken to the airport, where a private jet was waiting to take me back to Bermuda. The entourage that took me consisted of six cars and I was in the back of one of them squashed between armed police. They were taking no chances, they saw me as a very slippery person. To be honest, they were right. I had grown up with a built-in reaction to opportunities. If I had seen a chance of escape I probably would have taken it.

So there we were on a private jet in a private part of the airport with two armed police from Bermuda and one armed officer from Jamaica. These were my companions for the three-and-a-half-hour flight to Bermuda. They didn't say much and neither did I, but at least the seats were comfortable and I was going home.

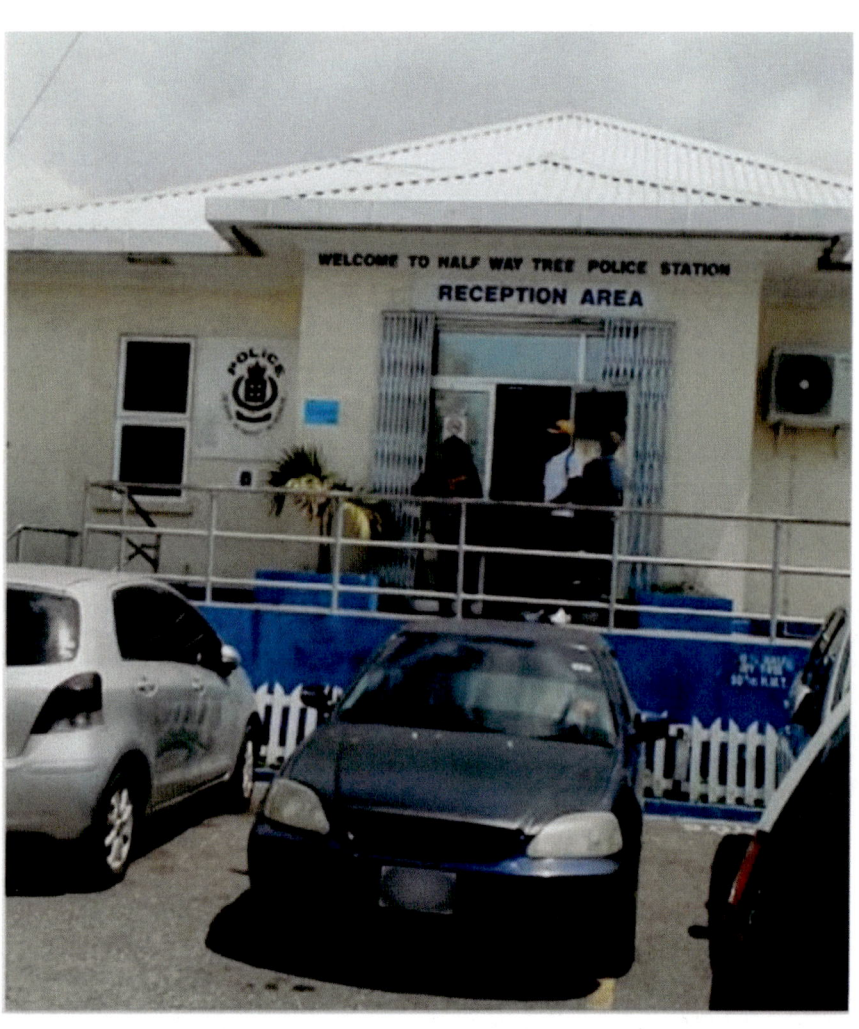

10: NO COMMENT!

Back in Bermuda again! I had mixed feelings when the plane touched down. Part of me rejoiced when I saw Bermuda and part of me tightened up because I faced serious charges, and much as the law is supposed to be that you are innocent until proven guilty, quite often attitudes are exactly the opposite.

I couldn't believe that when I got off the plane there was a really big entourage of police. I looked around to see if a VIP had landed as well but no, all those armed police were just for me. It reminded me of how serious this whole matter had become, and that because I was on wanted posters somehow that seemed to make them think I was all the more dangerous. I absolutely wasn't but there was no way they were going to take my word for that.

Our entourage arrived at the Bermuda Police Headquarters in Prospect Camp, which was a former military camp and still felt like it. Once in there I went straight to an interview room – they were keen to keep up the momentum. I was in there with several officers who started asking me questions. I learned from my past legal people that the only real option was to say "No comment" until you had some legal advisor next to you. They were frustrated of course, but that didn't worry me too much.

Things changed a little and the officers got a little excited when another officer came into the room holding an evidence bag. In it was a Tech9 machine gun. He showed it to me and then asked the classic question – "Does this belong to you?" I took my time in looking at it and then looked him in the eye and said, "No comment." I had to stop myself smiling when I saw how they all reacted the same – they slumped back in their seats – hopes smashed.

Immediately after that, I was taken to Hamilton police station and put in a cell in a line with other cells. A police officer sat on a chair immediately outside my cell.

"Why are you sitting there?" Some of the other inmates began asking him, partly goading him and partly because they wanted to know if I was some very dangerous criminal. Some of them actually knew me from street days but they still wanted to know. It was all starting to get even more bizarre. The presence of the police officer was an unpleasant experience for many of my fellow inmates, they felt stifled by his presence. I didn't really care one way or the other.

The word was 'Bulford's back' and my status grew. Let me go on record as saying that while that slightly amused me because it was so ridiculous, I did not enjoy it at all. I was not in the business of becoming some kind of gangster superstar. I never had ambitions like that, it was more of an embarrassment than anything else.

It did not help when I went to court two days later to be charged. My lawyer Richard Hector had been to see me and was unhappy that when he arrived I was in segregation. He asked why that was – had I caused any trouble? Had I threatened anyone? The answers were of course "No", so he had me moved back to a normal cell, although it was in the maximum security area.

BERMUDA TRIANGLE'S MOST WANTED

It was three weeks later that I had to go to court to be formally charged. I had been in jail all this time with armed guards constantly watching me. The day I went back to court was a drama all of its own. I was woken up at 5.30 am and given about 45 minutes to take a bath, prepare myself, have some breakfast and be ready to go. I wondered why we were leaving so early. Before we left for court the officers wanted me to put on a bullet-proof vest. I objected as I did not see the need, especially as I was being guarded and transported by an army of armed police. They forced me to put the vest on and put it on backward. I had to show them the correct way of wearing it. It is worth noting that I was the first prisoner to be escorted in this manner.

When I got outside, again there was an entourage of vehicles and a small army of armed police. Once in the vehicle we hit the road and traveled at speed through my old district. There was no stopping for red lights or anything else, and the reason we had left so early was that they wanted to miss the rush hour, which would have slowed us down. I later learned that one of the worries was that I had friends who would try to get me out of the police clutches. I probably did but I had no knowledge of any such exercise. We traveled so fast that we actually did in 11 minutes what might have taken more than half an hour normally.

In the background my solicitor had been working really hard and really well for me. So at the pre-trial hearing he had demanded, I was initially charged with possession of a firearm. The person who had handed in the gun told the court that he could not remember anything.

That was great news because no evidence meant that I could not really be charged with anything. So the firearm charge was dropped, much to my relief of course. I never really did find out the whole story, but one thing I was very sure of was that I was not involved in any way.

So there was no charge and I was free to go. I didn't hesitate. That was in May 2005 and I walked away from the court to start life again. I was not sorry.

A lot of well-meaning family friends told me to stay out of trouble. That was good advice of course but I didn't ever look for trouble, it always came looking for me!

My big question was simply now what? I had had enough of being stared at so I decided to keep a low profile for as long as possible. That is not easy when you are a tall guy and everyone has seen your photo all over the island. So yes, I did go back to street business but I kept as quiet as possible, and usually had someone else doing the actual trading for me. At least they posters had been taken down when I returned to Bermuda, but people still remember them.

One of my problems was that so many people knew me and if they saw me they wanted to have freedom to chat away to me, take photos and so on. Some of the policemen knew me, and they came and stood or sat with me while telling me how their family was.

So I was now going nowhere, a free man but without much prospect for the future. I didn't really want to have a business on the streets any more.

I decided it was time to have a legitimate business and make it grow. I guess I was starting to dream because it wasn't over yet. There were still some questions to be answered and even though I tried to put all that behind me, the police had other ideas.

11: NOT AGAIN!

I thought things were settling down at last, and that I could put the past behind me and move on. I was wrong of course, as in 2008 my world tipped upside down again. Where I was living was a fairly quiet neighborhood and most people knew each other.

I started noticing a car parked outside my house. Nothing strange about that except that there were two police officers in it, which told me that it was an unmarked police car and that could only mean one thing – surveillance. How did I know they were police officers? Instinct – you just know.

I shrugged it off and then went shopping for some food. I kept thinking about that car though, and then as I was riding back, from a distance I could see more police cars that looked as if they were outside my house. I rode the rest of the way anxious, and I was right to be. There was a whole pack of police trying to get into my house. They had a dog with them too, so they meant business – and a locksmith! I had a vault in the house with about $60,000 in it. The locksmith helped them open it and they took my money, along with some gold. It was later described as a gold bar. They also took two plumbing pipes found under my bed, and claimed that it meant I had been storing illegal drugs.

Time for the solicitor again. Two or three weeks later I had to reappear at the police station. They had done their forensics on the pipes and proved beyond doubt that they had been used at some stage for storing an illegal drug. My solicitor said that I could not be charged because there was no knowing what the pipes had been used for, and even if there were traces of something that could have been there long before they came into my possession.

However, I was still charged with possession of drug equipment and given bail until my trial. Almost one year later my trail began. In the middle of my trial my house was busted again, this time due to my alleged involvement in a kidnapping. Before the police actually got to my house my cousin had come to warn me. I was taking a shower and I remember thinking, the police have come to arrest me with my cock out AGAIN. They came to arrest me for this situation with full force: gun squad and military personnel. They knew that if given any chance to escape I would certainly take it. My windows and doors were broken as they attempted to gain entry to my home. Finally I was arrested and taken into custody.

After being held in the police station for a few days it was time for my trial to resume. Initially they did not allow me to be released so I could attend court. My lawyer had to go to court and get the judge to demand my presence so that I could finish my trial for the drug equipment. I was found guilty and sentenced to one year of imprisonment. I appealed of course, and my sentence was found to be excessive and reduced to six months. I had already served most of it, and had one month left on my sentence.

However, this still did not satisfy me. I knew I was innocent and I wanted my record cleared. I appealed again, and three judges from overseas heard the appeal and quashed the conviction. At last I was able to get out of there, get my money and gold back, and get on with life.

Dream on.

On the day of my release I was arrested again for my alleged involvement in the kidnapping. My co-accused were also rearrested. After being held for two days we were finally taken to court. The police could not actually pin it on us so they had to bring into play something called a noley. What this means is they drop their charge or interest but can change their minds within a year. We were given $20,000 bail under the condition that we checked in three times week. This lasted for at least a year.

12: TRYING TO PROVE MY INNOCENCE

I was not alone in this charge – my cousin and a pal had also been implicated and rearrested. I had better explain what exactly the charge was. We were jointly charged with abducting a guy called Dwayne Reid-Anderson, who had dual Jamaican and Bermudan citizenship, and holding him against his will as well as causing him harm with a firearm and attempting to steal $4,000 from him.

For what it is worth, you have my word that it was complete nonsense.

So we were arrested and appeared in court the next day. Our lawyers put up a good case for us to be bailed. The judge had the good sense to see that our lawyers were right in their assessment that we were not a danger to society, and agreed to set bail at $5,000.

That was just the start of an amazing story. My lawyer asked for a pretrial hearing and produced some further evidence which he hoped would make the whole thing look ridiculous. First of all he was able to reveal that the guy had himself been in police custody facing a number of charges.

I learned that a lot of lawyers had come to witness this trial because it had gathered a lot of publicity and also because they felt they could learn something. They were right, they could – and many of them later said that they did. I really did hope so because it was all rather bizarre as far as I was concerned, and I genuinely hoped others would not go through the same torment in the future. Next came the news that the guy had actually absconded and run off to Jamaica. He was not even there to give evidence.

The prosecution wanted to go ahead anyway as they had sheets of statements he had made before he disappeared. So it looked as if we were going to full trial. The judge was given all the statements to review and it was pointed out to her by the lawyer of one of my co-defendants that there was a page missing. The judge asked for it to be produced before the hearing.

We naturally continued to plead our innocence – why wouldn't we? At the eventual hearing the statement had still not appeared and the judge at Hamilton CMC – Judge Charles-Etta Simmons – actually called the prosecutor to take the stand and then quizzed him over the missing statement.

It turned out that the piece missing was actually vital and really proved that the whole case was without foundation. The guy who claimed that we had done these things refused to return to Bermuda and said he had made up the whole story just to cause some trouble for us. We barely knew him. The papers followed the whole story and wrote, "According to the ruling from Justice Simmons, police received a report "regarding a firearm" and found Reid-Anderson in an "injured state" on a road in Pembroke parish. He received hospital treatment but refused to tell officers what happened, beyond saying the incident arose over a chain.

"After he was taken to a safe house, he told police in an interview that the three defendants forced him to accompany them to the scene, beat him over the head with a gun and bound him with rope. However, prosecutors dropped the charges against them after Reid-Anderson withdrew his complaint in the case."

Assistant Police Commissioner David Mirfield said the Bermuda Police Service respected the decision of the court, but that the choice to prosecute had been the correct one.

Clearly not. The judge was clearly disgusted by the missing statement and took the view that this was deliberately done so that we had little defense.

The officer in charge of the case had been exposed. He seemed determined to get us convicted no matter what evidence he did or did not have. As the evidence stacked up more and more in our favor, he started to get very jittery. It struck me that he was prepared to try anything to get my head. It had become personal and I did not want to go down that route. It was not because of fear or anything like that, I just did not want to engage with someone who was prepared to bend the rules like that for his own ends.

To make sure that there was no ambiguity, the judge instructed the jury to return formal not guilty verdicts on all counts on the grounds that it would be unfair for us to stand trial without the accuser or his correct statement being available. That made sure that we could not be taken back to court to answer the same case.

Shadow Justice Minister Trevor Moniz told reporters that Reid-Anderson should be made to pay for the aborted case. Asked for his view on the matter, Moniz said: "It is unfortunately a very good illustration of the problems we face.

One thing that comes to mind is whether complainants need to face sanctions for the cost of public time and money. Someone should be going after this guy and saying 'you have cost us all this money and you should pay it back. This money could have been better spent on something else."

So, we were free men and that felt so good after all the hassle and worry. Sometimes you wonder if you will ever recover from all that stress and the stigma attached to accusations, even when you have been proven innocent.

It is not just police and legal matters. Life itself seems to kick you in the teeth for no particular reason and sometimes you are not the actual victim but share the sadness of what has happened.

A classic example was when we were out celebrating the 24th birthday of a friend of mine one evening in 1995. We were travelling to a venue in several different cars and one of them was involved in a crash, a serious crash. My friend was in that car with a group of our other friends. The car flipped and his neck was broken. It was awful. I couldn't believe that my good friend had died on his 24th birthday because of an accident. None of us will ever forget it or him.

It just goes to show that even when you have done nothing wrong you can be victim and for those around you their lives are altered for something they never did.

That chapter closed and it was time to get back to business, never again to fall foul of the law. The trouble is that these incidents can stay with you for life – deservedly or not.

There is always a lot of media coverage and of course, I had had my picture previously plastered all over the papers, and even though they had since been taken down there were previously posters of me on noticeboards, in shop windows, on walls and even on trees, so getting a low profile once again was not going to be a walk in the park.

A lot of people knew me because they had seen my picture in the media, but I was quite determined that my life was not going to remain like that. Yes I had to live with the stigma for a while, but hopefully not forever. Some people even saw me as some kind of celebrity but that is not what I wanted for myself.

I had a fishing business which I could develop in to something special, and I could still operate Crown and Anchor, which I will talk more about later. Perfectly legitimate businesses and no need for me to cross swords with the police ever again.

If only…

13: MORE ARRESTS!

Sometimes it seems that the more you try to go straight and put your crimes behind you, the more difficult it becomes. Even the most innocent action you take can be held against you because you have gained a reputation and even if that reputation is only for petty crime, other people can turn it into legendary status. That happened to me when I traveled on one of the charter flights to Jamaica around 2007.

One of the police in Bermuda saw me getting onto the flight and he kindly phoned through to Montego Bay Airport to ensure that I would get a warm welcome. It's hard to get any other kind at Montego Bay!

Sure enough when the plane touched down I was met by my old friend Biggerford of the Jamaican police. He arrested me straight away, saying that I was not allowed to be there. With the help of the airport police – not that he needed any help as I was passive and had seen it all before, of course – we went to the police headquarters and I was asked what I was doing in Jamaica.

I told them the truth, that I was on vacation. Some of my friends were with me and a police officer asked their names and then phoned through to Bermuda to see if they were wanted for anything. Two of the other guys were accused of having fake passports but that was totally untrue. It was clear that they were trying to find something to justify their actions.

At one point we were searched and patted down. Since I had some money strapped to my leg just below the knee they didn't do a very good job. The money was just for spending on holiday but past experience told me not to let anyone see that I was carrying a large amount of cash, because they automatically wanted to prove that it was for some illegal reason – which it wasn't – or they would try to steal it.

Not satisfied that they were getting nowhere they decided on another search – this time it was to be a strip search and I had to pull my pants down. I lowered them as far as my knees and then they told me to get dressed. They still had not seen my spending money.

I was taken to the police headquarters in Kingston and there was quite a sight to behold when I walked in, as there was a guy laying on the floor and handcuffed to the leg of a desk. I didn't know whether to laugh or be alarmed.

It turned out that he had tried to make a run for it so they had wrestled him to the ground and handcuffed him to the furniture. He was going nowhere and I was starting to know how he felt.

I realized that I should phone my lawyer but it was Sunday and I couldn't get through to him. So they put me in a cell for the night with two Jamaicans and a Colombian, all harmless. I was searched again and still they found nothing. I realized that having that money on me and being in a cell with other guys was not a great scenario so I stayed awake until they seemed to have fallen asleep, then unstrapped the money and hid it in my bundle of clothes which was right by me.

I managed to get some sleep and the next morning I called my lawyer, who told them they had no grounds for keeping me and I must be allowed to go.

It is worth mentioning that in Jamaica there is an unofficial name for a more ruthless type of policeman. They are called Kingfish, and they believe that rules apply to other people. I met plenty of them in my time. They all know each other and they stick together. I am not saying that Biggerford and the others were in this category but I didn't know that they were not.

My release was delayed for a couple more hours and then two officers were assigned to get me to the airport so that I could catch a plane to Montego Bay. It was a pleasant drive to Tinson Pen Aerodrome and I gave the two officers a $100 bill each as a tip. There was a lady on the phone at the reception desk and it was clear she was talking about me. Now what?

Nothing. She just knew someone in Bermuda and they were comparing notes and all was well. At last I was able to get onto the plane which was a small, private passenger jet and we took off. Holiday at last!

The first place I went after my release was to a local brothel. I needed to relieve some built-up stress. My friends and I got the women we were interested in and headed out for a night of partying. My night ended with myself and two females having an orgy, or as I call it, fun. I remember sitting back drinking my Chivas on the rocks, smoking my spliff watching these women pleasure each other thinking all that stress was totally worth it. In that moment I felt like a king. I was finally relaxed and enjoying my company. It was a good night indeed!

So, that was the end of my brushes with the law. I wish I could say that but it wouldn't be true. There was more to come of course.

In 2010 I had two more incidents which were nothing to do with me but I was there. On the first occasion I was at a party in Woody's Sports Bar in Sandys and met up with an old friend of mine, Freddie Maybury. We were not close friends but knew each other quite well as we were from the same neighborhood. We chatted a bit but didn't stay together for the evening. The party was good and everyone seemed to be having a good time.

At one stage I was talking to two girls and all was well and the next thing I heard multiple gun shots coming from the other side of the building. There was a lot of screaming, running for cover and total mayhem. People were getting into cars, onto motorbikes, anything that would get them away from what was happening. I heard someone say, "He's been shot!" I didn't know who they were talking about for a while and then I realized that it was Freddie. He died that night.

It was not the only one that year though, as I was there when a guy called Randy Lightbourne was shot. That was another party and I was sitting in an outdoor area at Somerset's Charing Cross Tavern. It was early evening, about 5pm, and I had just got some food. There was a party going on but I had my back to it. Suddenly I heard a motorbike which sounded like it was going to run into the building but it stayed in the parking lot. Then I heard multiple shots and well-known local career criminal and police informant Randy Lightbourne was hit.

It was chaos of course. I couldn't imagine it being anything else when there is a gunman cutting loose. Unfortunately, Randy Lightbourne survived. I had just pinned myself down alongside a wall and kept out of the way.

Strangely when the matter went to court, Randy Lightbourne gave evidence and actually mentioned my name in connection with the whole thing. Randy Ratbourne labeled me as the leader of a local gang "mob" and suggested that I was the mastermind behind the incident. Luckily for me he was known to police and his word could not be trusted, so it did not hold any weight in court, I am glad to say. After his case he was taken away into police custody. From what I hear he is now a child of the Lord, a pastor... Imagine.

It just goes to show though, that even when you are trying to put your past behind you there is always someone that will drag it up. I guess the answer is not to get involved in the first place.

14: WINNING BIG 73K

July 1, 2012 was the day lady luck was on my side. In the summer of 2012 the European Football Championship was held. I have always been a fan of Italy and this particular year Italy made it to the semi-finals. Excited about our position in the tournament I decided to place multiple bets on the semi-final game against Germany. Being an avid soccer fan, betting is something I engaged in frequently in my neighborhood with friends, but this time I decided to place it with local betting shop Seahorses. I placed two bets with them: Italy to win with a score of 2-1, with a returning stake of $25,000, and for Italy player Mario Balotelli to score within the 90 minutes with a returning stake of $18,000. Apart from these two, I had multiple bets on the semi-finals with my friends for various amounts ranging from $1,000-$10,000, and totaling $30,000. I guess you can say I had the upmost faith in my team.

The day of the semi-finals I remember I woke up feeling optimistic about the game. I got dressed in my Italy jersey and carried my Italy flag, ready to represent my team to the fullest. With my air horn and flag in hand I decided to watch the game at a local sports bar Woody's. The energy around the bar was exciting and encouraging. Everyone was amped up having a good time cheering on their respective teams. Finally, the game started, it was tight, both teams played good football. Although Italy had majority possession of the ball my anxiety warmed up. I needed Balotelli to score and Italy to win 2-1. Then in the 20th minute he scored! My excitement was uncontainable – I had just won $18,000 in 20 minutes! Thank you, Balotelli. The game progressed and then Balotelli scored again in the 36th minute. The game continued with both teams having multiple chances to score with no success. On one hand my team was winning but on the other hand I needed Germany to score to ensure a score of 2-1 to Italy. As the 90th minute was approaching I became increasingly nervous, willing a Germany goal. Now I was pacing up and down from inside to outside. My opponents were upset and I was nervous. The energy around the bar had shifted completely and silence descended as everyone awaited the final whistle. Then boom, Germany were given a penalty in the 92nd minute. What are the odds!? I couldn't fucking believe it! I jumped from my seat and ran outside in excitement, almost jumping into the ocean celebrating what I hoped would become a goal. I was so anxious I couldn't bring myself to watch the penalty. I stayed outside awaiting the result, until finally someone came outside shouting "They scored"! At this point I was no more good, I was running up and down shouting with pure joy and excitement. I ran back in, arrogant and excited. I had just won $25,000! I rang the bell at the bar – in Bermuda when someone rings the bar bell everyone at the bar gets a drink on their tab. I had just won $73,000 in 90 minutes, surely I could afford a few drinks. I threw all the cash I had with me all over the bar for the bartender, it had to be at least $2,000. It rained $5s and $10s that day, the entire floor behind the bar was covered in money. In that moment I was daddy! Bar staff told me in the following days that they were still finding money around the bar. The barmaid was tipped well that day.

Two days later I went to collect my winnings. I was given a check for $18,000 and was asked to return the following week to collect the remainder of my winnings. I was OK with this pay-out system, as my winnings were huge. I deposited my check into my bank account and awaited my next collection date. In between collecting my winnings from Seahorses I had collected $30,000 in winnings from bets made with friends from my neighborhood. Finally, the day arrived and I was able to collect my final payment from Seahorses. I got my check, thanked them and headed straight to the bank to deposit my winnings. But as luck would have it, two days later I received a call from a friend saying that the owner of Seahorses had been asking who Kenith Bulford was. Apparently, officers from the Financial Crimes Unit were investigating my bets. It was suggested that I was using the betting shop to clean my money obtained by criminal activity. Here we go again! My first time betting using a betting shop, I win and suddenly something criminal has to be involved. However, all attempts to criminalize my winnings failed and no charges were brought forth.

Three weeks later and $73,000 richer, I planned a shopping spree for myself. As I was attempting to leave Bermuda I was held up at the airport and all the cash I had on me was seized, approximately $9.500. All without a valid reason. Even with this negative turn of events, I still went on my trip. I will deal with this when I get back, I thought. Upon my return I hired Victoria Pearman to represent me. We went to court and won the case, and my money was returned. In my opinion, the police only seized my money at the airport because they were bitter about not being able to touch the money I had recently won – it felt personal.

July 1st 2012, one of the luckiest days of my life. $73,000 in 90 minutes.

15: CROWN AND ANCHOR

As I mentioned a few chapters ago, I loved playing Crown and Anchor and had done for many years. For those of you who have never encountered it before, Crown and Anchor is basically a board game between two players, one of whom is the banker. How it works is that the player places bets on one or more symbols and three dice are placed into a dark cup, shaken and turned over on the table. If there is a bet on any symbol which comes up on one or more of the dice, the banker returns the player's stake on that symbol, and additionally pays out the value of that stake for each die showing that symbol. If it doesn't the banker wins.

In a private game the two players would change roles periodically, but when it is a public game – and a very popular one – the banker is always the one who owns the game. My mother taught me all the ins and outs of Crown and Anchor and showed me that it is a good thing to be the banker, just like being a bookmaker.

She loaned me some money to get a good edition of the game and I started to have my own table at County cricket games, which always drew good support. In the early days of doing that I remember one Saturday at a cricket match it was really busy, and at the end of the day I had made a couple of thousand dollars. It was all totally legal too.

At a big cup match which was also a public holiday I also took a lot of money. It was all fair so I had a new business and it was working well. I decided to expand it and to do that I started taking bigger bets. Most boards only took small bets, but for the really keen players I provided the facility for higher stakes. The biggest single bet I took was $9,500 on one single symbol. To keep the excitement around my boards I would often switch it up by using only one dice, or take bets on the side. I would even give every female that played on my table their first bet for free.

Then I doubled the business by operating two boards at once, and even arranged for a set of TVs around the boards so that my customers could also watch sport, music videos or whatever they wanted while still playing Crown and Anchor. I called it the Megaboard and I was the first person to do that. The customers loved it – and so did I.

My popularity from Cup Match and Crown and Anchor meant more attraction to my other business. I used to charter my two boats for parties during the summer. After Cup Match there is usually a big boat raft up called Non-Mariners. I would always have my boats rented out or full of females I had met during Cup Match at my Crown and Anchor table. These boat parties often turned explicit due to the rum, fun and sun. If only I could talk about some of my adventures.

Even that did not run totally smoothly, because in 2012 the police closed me down. I had a nearly three-year court battle to get my business back but eventually I did, because I had not been doing anything illegal.

During this time, in March 2013, myself and two friends were detained at Bermuda's main airport because we had a lot of cash with us. When I tell you that it amounted to

$325,000 you will easily understand why it was hidden in the luggage, with about $10,000 dollars on me personally.

It is an international problem that luggage is often 'lost' or has been opened and things gone missing as that luggage is moved from plane to plane or to a main airport building. It happens all the time, so when you are moving your personal savings you take every precaution.

As with many people in Bermuda and other parts of the world, I was brought up in a culture of cash not banking technology, so when I decided that it would be good to move to the UK for more than just a holiday or family visits, I wanted to take my savings with me.

When I was asked about the money, I explained that and said that my friends were just helping me. I told them that it was all perfectly legitimate earnings from Crown and Anchor and my fishing business, and I had worked hard to obtain it.

They wouldn't believe me and once again I was faced with going to court. I took the stand in my defense. My lawyer Larry Mussenden was also in disbelief as he could not believe that I was being accused of money laundering. When the case finally came to the Supreme Court he explained things perfectly and in no time the jury found me not guilty. It took him less than two weeks to prove the case

I was told I was free to go by Puisne Judge Juan Wolffe and Larry told the *Royal Gazette* newspaper, "I want to thank the jury for their consideration and for returning unanimous not guilty verdicts. It is clear that the evidence in this case was extremely weak from the start, and I am surprised that the Crown brought this case against Mr Bulford. I will have to take instructions from my client with regards to the money which has been found by the jury's verdict not to be the proceeds of crime. In my view, he is entitled to have all these funds returned to him."

Amazingly, during the trial, prosecutors said that I was a high-ranking member of a West End gang and was involved in the importation and supply of drugs. They alleged that I had earned the $325,000 seized at the airport from crime and that I had been trying to smuggle the cash to Britain. Needless to say, under oath I denied all that and explained the whole truth and nothing but the truth of the situation.

Larry also said that the police had got it all wrong and added, "In respect of the gang evidence of Sergeant Rollin, I objected to this officer being considered an expert in this case. I am of the view that he does not qualify as a gang expert in this case or in any other case. Equally so for Detective Sergeant Bhagwan, who was tendered as an expert on drugs in Bermuda and overseas. I objected to his expertise when it came to overseas jurisdictions. I believe the verdicts back up my objections."

So I walked away a free man but then had another fight to get back my money, which they had confiscated. I also had to fight to get permission to resume Crown and Anchor.

At last when the hearing finally took place the judge could not see why I had been stopped, and I was allowed to go back into business again – just in time for another big public holiday.

I was delighted of course, but still apprehensive that something else might cause trouble. I was beginning to think that there was someone with a list of crimes and every time I was in trouble they just ticked off that crime and moved on to another one, whether it had actually happened or not!

None of that changed my love of Crown and Anchor, and to this day I still operate tables now and then – all legal and all fun. You win some and you lose some – in the money-laundering court case we won but I was not about to accept the loss of my hard-earned money, which remained confiscated even though I was innocent. The battle was not over yet.

16: WHAT HAPPENED NEXT?

Well, I should perhaps have been grateful that no case was proven and that I could have another fresh start to life. But the truth is that despite my clear innocence, a lot of my money – my savings – had been illegally confiscated. This was money I had earned from the fishing business I had owned for some years while all these other crazy things were going on.

What would you have done? A jury had unanimously found me not guilty of possessing proceeds of crime. I had been given back just over $10,000 but not the $314,950 because it had 'already been forfeited'. Not by me!

My lawyer, Jerome Lynch, asked the court to set aside the forfeiture order, which I had known nothing about. The complication was that one of the two ladies who were travelling with me at the time caved in to pressure and put in a plea of guilty and agreed to forfeit the money. That was totally crazy. We were innocent as proven and it was not her money to forfeit! I knew nothing about it until the deed was done and therefore I had had no opportunity to put in an objection. I had no idea what had happened.

Mr Justice Hargun, the judge, said "I am satisfied that the court was in possession of sufficient material in relation to the potential interest of Mr Buford in the funds, and that he should have been given notice so as to allow him to make any representations to the court he considered appropriate. In any event, having regard to the fact that Mr Bulford maintains in sworn evidence that he was wholly unaware of the forfeiture proceedings and that he has been denied an opportunity to make representations to the court, in relation to his interests in the funds, he should be afforded such an opportunity."

Well, I could not bring myself to walk away from what was truly my money, the results of my accumulated business earnings. What would happen to it anyway?

So I set the legal proceedings in place. I lost the forfeiture case and refuse to appeal again, as the costs are astronomical. It has been a few years now and miles of words on paper, but as I write this I am no nearer getting repaid and I wonder if I ever will. Probably not. That said, there is absolutely no reason why I should not get my money back.

Sometimes I wonder whose side justice favors.

Life goes on though, and as far as I am aware there is no reason why I should be looking over my shoulder at airports. I have family and friends in Britain so I travel there a few times a year and I don't find myself being hounded.

Back in Bermuda, everything has calmed down for me. I still see some of the same people – it is not a big island. Everyone knows that the past is past, and these days I do my best not to do anything wrong or give anyone any excuse to think that I might do.

When I look back at the various things that have happened, I am amazed to find myself still alive. I am grateful for that, the alternative is not good.

I am also amazed at how my getting involved in small crime somehow led to me being accused of all kinds of other, much bigger crimes. It is not something you really think about when you are a kid running errands for people on the streets. You are just thrilled to be earning a little bit of money and associating with the big boys.

Even when things move up a grade and you do a bit of dealing of your own, you still don't look beyond the day. Remember that there was also a period when we sold cool clothes from the States and I guess that those of us who were selling drugs just saw it as another hustle. Clothes, drugs, seafood – what did it matter just so long as at the end of that day you had more money in your pocket than you started with and you could afford to buy something to eat.

That is how it was for me. The pleasure came in having some money and hanging out with people that you looked up to. Looking back, maybe there were other people I should have looked up to but you can't turn back the clock.

I certainly never expected all the complications that came later, getting arrested time after time and being in the frame for some serious stuff. How did that happen? It is what happens when you have your feet in the pool, you never know when something in the water is going to come and bite you, something that is nothing to do with you – you didn't put it there but because your feet were in the water you were involved.

I was a little kid when I first got involved and now I am almost 50, and I have learned a few things.

One of those things is how to earn an honest living. There is nothing illegal about Crown and Anchor and nothing illegal about fishing. Both were part of my past and there was no reason why they should not be part of my legal future.

It seemed to me to be a good idea that if the police started asking, "Where's Bulford?", someone else would be able to reply, "Gone Fishin'."

17: GONE FISHING - AND GOING STRAIGHT

This is probably a good time to mention that for all these years my real desire was to lead a normal life, or as normal as it gets in Bermuda. I love the place and the people. If you have never been, let me tell you that it is considered one of the most beautiful places on the planet.

Horseshoe Bay is known throughout the world as something that you might call paradise. The water is clean and always warm, and the beaches are the kind of thing that travel agents like to have photos of all over their walls. Today the living facilities are so much better, but that does not detract from its beauty.

As anywhere else in the world, it helps if you have some money, but the cost of living for ordinary people is not out of reach. The wildlife is great and varied both in and out of the ocean. The social life is great and really it is just an ideal place to live.

So why do I and people like me feel the need to go to Jamaica, the US and Britain for breaks? Well, Bermuda is not very big and when you live there all the time you start to take things for granted a little. So if you stretch your legs and go somewhere else for a while, you appreciate it all the more when you come home.

I wanted nothing more than to live peacefully and have a couple of businesses that would keep me ahead of the game.

I had inherited a love of fishing from my grandfather so that was an obvious road for me to travel down. I loved it and I knew enough about it to make it work for me.

I have the fishing business right now and sometimes I go out and other times I have people who help me. I usually go out at about six or seven in the morning and probably stay out until the afternoon. There is never a need to go too far out into the ocean, because the fishing restrictions mean there is plenty to be caught if everyone plays by the same rules, which mostly they do.

I usually catch rockfish, snappers and other medium-size fish, but occasionally we will find a barracuda in the net. As we haul them in we set to work straight away preparing them for sale so that by the time we get back to shore we can supply our customers fish that are truly very fresh.

We have sales points just by our mooring places. People come and buy as soon as they know we are in, and we also have regular customers who buy the same kind of fish most of the time. By the time the day has ended we have made some money. There are quite good profits but, of course, you have to make sure that your boat and your equipment is always up to standard. We keep a constant eye on the weather too. Our boats are not the huge trawlers that stay at sea for months and have refrigeration plants and other facilities. By our standards we are quite modern, but really we are not too far away from the kind of fishing that has been done by Bermudian families for generations.

We see big turtles quite often, an occasional shoal of jellyfish, and now and then a great white shark will enter our waters. They don't stay for very long, they are not very interested in what we have to offer.

I enjoy the fishing and I still enjoy attending big cricket matches and other events. Without wishing to sound like the Head of Tourism for Bermuda, it really is a beautiful place to live, and there are a number of people from other parts of the world who have bought homes here and stay regularly. The general atmosphere in Bermuda is pretty relaxed and – apart from the occasional hurricane – the weather is pretty good all the time.

As for me, well I am still well-known in Bermuda, especially in the area where I grew up. I still get the police keeping an eye on me just in case. I don't blame them for being suspicious, that is their job, but it would be nice to have the benefit of the doubt without having to prove myself quite so much.

I get time with my family now of course, and there is no time I like better. I grew up with family all around me and I still enjoy that the most.

The journey to get here has been full of stress and I don't really have too much of that any more, I guess I smile a lot more these days. Why not? After all, I am a regular guy these days.

What have I learned and what is the point of this book? On reflection, I didn't do even half of the things I was accused of, but I did take up a lifestyle that was not the best, so I couldn't blame anyone for assuming that if I did this thing then I could be suspected of doing that thing, even if it was much worse.

I couldn't say that I enjoyed fleeing from country to country but it taught me to live on my wits, and there are few problems I face now that I am not equipped to resolve fairly quickly. That makes it sound as if I am recommending any young person to get an education on the streets, do things the way I did and you will be able to deal with the rest of what life throws at you.

No, quite the opposite. Learn to use your wits and tackle problems head on but do your best to stay legal and don't put yourself in a situation where you can be arrested just because you have a bit of a reputation. Don't put yourself in a situation where guns are likely to be fired at a party. Trust me, that's not fun. Get yourself a regular business – do some fishing, sell some clothes from the States, make a million dollars but think legal, it really is the best choice.

So, here I am sitting in the sun and looking over the sea, it is looking good. I am not fishing today but I will have some time with family and friends. I am now the proud father of several children and have lost numerous friends to death or jail.

There are some things I regret, of course. There are some things I don't regret but they are mostly the fun things.

I wonder if any of those policemen who arrested me just because I was there have any regrets? I know I do.

So I sit here, an honest citizen with honest means of income. I keep fairly busy with those things but sometimes, just sometimes, I do get kinda bored.

IN CONCLUSION

So, here we are at the end of the story so far. I said at the beginning that this was not to glorify me or what I have been doing with my life, but there is a point to this.

Was I guilty of murder? Absolutely not!
Was I guilty of kidnapping? Absolutely not!
Was I guilty of money-laundering? Absolutely not!

All the above were proven, and I am a free man and a successful businessman because I have put these things behind me.

Was I totally innocent then? Absolutely not!

In telling my story I have explained where I went wrong and why I went wrong. I learned my lessons the hard way and paid for what I did wrong. One of the problems that are largely unseen though is those frightening times when you are accused of really serious crimes of which you are innocent. You know you are innocent and so do those who are really guilty, but the very fact that you have run with the pack, associated with people who have committed greater crimes than your own, makes you an automatic target for suspicion. The police mark you and you are likely to be rounded up at any time, even if you were nowhere near the crime scene.

I wouldn't wish my dark experiences on anyone but the trap is open for anyone to fall into. As a kid growing up in the environment in which I did, there are not many opportunities open to you to do more than scrape a living. So it is very tempting when someone asks you to take something from A to B and pays you well for it. You don't care what you are carrying or why, you just see it as some cash in your pocket or maybe, if you are really ambitious, as a step towards that new suit you crave, that car that will impress the girls. The trouble is that once you have run that first errand with something in your pocket that your employer doesn't want to be caught with, you have just taken your first steps into a life of suspicion, constantly looking over your shoulder and maybe putting yourself in a position in which you might find yourself being arrested as a murder suspect.

I'm clean now. I have a fishing business and I play Crown and Anchor. When I am not doing that, I am relaxed having time with friends without fear of being arrested for something I know nothing about. I can get on a plane and visit my family and friends in Britain.

The whole point of this book, then, is that what I have now is what I wish for other people. I have revealed my errors in the hope that people will realize that they could make the same mistakes and it might not turn out so well for them.

I love Bermuda, and I love my family and friends who are all part of my story. I hope their path in life is the best possible and free of the errors that are now part of my past. They were an adventure, exciting sometimes – but I am happier now than I ever was then.

Kenith Bulford

Story Terrace

Made in the USA
Columbia, SC
17 December 2023

796670e2-ba9d-42e6-8d0e-d504b331fee9R01